Project Mercury: The History and Legacy of America's First Human Spaceflight Program

By Charles River Editors

Mercury Control Center at Cape Canaveral

About Charles River Editors

Charles River Editors provides superior editing and original writing services in the digital publishing industry, with the expertise to create digital content for publishers across a vast range of subject matter. In addition to providing original digital content for third party publishers, we also republish civilization's greatest literary works, bringing them to new generations of readers via ebooks.

Sign up here to receive updates about free books as we publish them, and visit Our Kindle Author Page to browse today's free promotions and our most recently published Kindle titles.

Introduction

An Atlas rocket at Cape Canaveral

Project Mercury

"We're not up there in space just to joyride around. We're up there to do things that are of value to everybody right here on Earth." – John Glenn

Today the Space Race is widely viewed poignantly and fondly as a race to the Moon that culminated with Apollo 11 "winning" the Race for the United States. In fact, it encompassed a much broader range of competition between the Soviet Union and the United States that affected everything from military technology to successfully launching satellites that could land on Mars or orbit other planets in the Solar System. Moreover, the notion that America "won" the Space Race at the end of the 1960s overlooks just how competitive the Space Race actually was in launching people into orbit, as well as the major contributions the Space Race influenced in leading to today's International Space Station and continued space exploration.

  The successful Apollo 11 mission was certainly an astonishing technological triumph, but what is less well remembered now are that many programs preceded Apollo and were essential to its success. Project Mercury was one of those, and in many ways it represented the greatest step forward in terms of the conquest of space. Before Project Mercury, there was no certainty that a human could survive the rigors of a space launch or live outside Earth's atmosphere. There was no agreement on just what an astronaut should be, and various individuals involved debated whether they should be pilots, technicians, scientists, or even merely observers in an automated craft. Before Project Mercury, no one was entirely certain what a rocket capable of taking a person into space would look like, or even whether building such a craft was within the capabilities of engineering in the 1950s.

Put simply, Project Mercury aimed to answer these and other questions while overcoming technological and human problems never before faced. All the while, the program took place against he backdrop of intense competition between the Soviets and the United States to be the first to be able to send people into space and, if possible, to use that for military advantage. Because of this, Project Mercury was not just a step into the unknown, but part of an ongoing battle taking place in the glare of constant publicity to allow America to catch up with what frequently looked like an unassailable lead in space by the USSR.

Project Mercury lasted for less than five years, but the missions were some of the most momentous and intense years in the history of space flight. When Project Mercury began in October 1958, no person had traveled to space and some people still believed that this was impossible. By the time that it ended in June 1963, the Apollo Program that would place an American on the Moon in 1969 had begun, but without Project Mercury, there could have been no Apollo Program.

Project Mercury: The History and Legacy of America's First Human Spaceflight Program examines the origins behind the missions, the people and spacecraft involved, and the historic results. Along with pictures of important people, places, and events, you will learn about Mercury like never before.

The Start of the Space Race

By the late 1950s, what was previously a race to deliver nuclear arms using space became a race for admission into space alone. Although the 1940s and early 1950s were necessarily dominated by a quest to create rockets for military use, the latter half of the 1950s saw the science and technology fueling the Space Race being advanced as part of a competition for political prestige between the two ideological adversaries.

Dovetailing off their success with intercontinental ballistic missiles (ICBMs), the Soviets were the first to make enormous advances in actual space exploration. On the night of October 4, 1957, the Soviets prepared to launch "Object D" atop one of its R-7 rockets. As the world's first ICBMs, R-7 rockets were built primarily to carry nuclear warheads, but "Object D" was a far different payload. "Object D" and the R-7 rocket launched from a hastily constructed launch pad, and within minutes it entered orbit. It took that object, now more famously known as Sputnik-1, about 90 minutes to complete its orbit around the Earth, speeding along at 18,000 miles per hour while transmitting a distinct beeping noise by radio.

Sputnik-1

Thanks to its transmission, and the bright mark it created in nighttime skies across the world, the world was already aware of the launch and orbit of Sputnik-1 before the Soviets formally announced the successful launch and orbit of their satellite. Naturally, the West wasn't thrilled to learn about the Soviets' launch of the first artificial object into Earth's orbit. Sputnik-1 could be measured in inches, but that large rocket it was attached to could wreak havoc if equipped with a nuclear warhead. Moreover, if Americans could see Sputnik-1, they were justifiably worried Sputnik-1 could see them.

The launch of Sputnik I is largely hailed as the opening moment of the true "Space Race", in part because of the fame and fear inspired by the launch, but also because its purpose was not entirely one of military value. While the Sputnik satellite indicated the Soviets had significant military advantages in potentially weaponizing space, Sputnik's value was not exclusively military. Internationally, the political reaction to the Sputnik launch was muted. President Eisenhower's White House was largely dismissive of the success, refusing to acknowledge its significance. Eisenhower played down the satellite, saying it was no surprise.

In truth, President Eisenhower immediately realized the implications posed by the Soviets' successful launch, and Sputnik-1 was a huge propaganda victory for the Soviets, who could boast not only of accomplishing the historic first but of getting ahead of the Americans in the Space Race. Had something like Sputnik-1 been America's goal in 1957, it very likely could have accomplished this important first. Wernher von Braun, a former Nazi scientist who became instrumental in America's space efforts, had successfully designed the Jupiter-C rocket by 1956, which could have allowed the United States to launch a satellite like Sputnik-1 into space a year before the Soviets did. At the time, however, the technology was being designed for use as missiles. In response to Sputnik-

1, Eisenhower quickly ordered an attempt to put a satellite in orbit, so a Space Race of a more civilian nature was launched.

Von Braun

Despite the importance Eisenhower placed on the Space Race in response to Sputnik-1, it would take years for NASA to fully catch up. In fact, before the United States could even craft a response to Sputnik-1, the Soviets launched Sputnik-2 on November 3, 1957, which carried an even more impressive payload into space. With Sputnik-2, the Soviets launched more than just an artificial satellite. For the first time, a living mammal – a dog named Laika – was launched into outer space. This invariably made America's previous launch of fruit flies seem utterly insignificant. Launching a dog into space represented a much bigger step along the path to sending a human being into space.

Laika

As a stray dog from Moscow, Laika seemed an unusual candidate to make history as the first living thing to orbit around the Earth. At that time, however, nobody was sure what effects space travel might have on the human body, and the Soviets weren't confident enough in their launching technology to risk their cosmonauts' lives. Thus, Laika and two other dogs trained for the Sputnik-2 mission, which included isolating the dogs and forcing them to live in cramped compartments.

Laika was the winner, but that didn't make her a lucky winner. Unbeknownst to the poor dog, she was given a suicide mission. In 1957, the Soviets had no clue how to de-orbit a spacecraft through reentry into the Earth's atmosphere, and they had no intention of trying to figure it out for a stray dog. It is still not entirely clear when or how the dog died during the mission; the Soviets later claimed she lived for days, either euthanized with poisoned food or dying when the oxygen onboard ran out, but it's now believed she died within hours from an overheated cabin.

Nevertheless, the mission was considered a wild success because Laika proved an animal could survive the launch and entry into space. Indeed, her journey was a momentous one and one of the most important in the history of space flight. Russian scientists were able to discern the effects of weightlessness and space travel on a living body, paving the way for the launch of a human into outer space.

On December 6, 1957, about two months after Sputnik-1, Americans were ready to watch the result of Project Vanguard, which would launch a Vanguard Test Vehicle 3 rocket from its launch pad at Cape Canaveral, Florida. The rocket was carrying a satellite much like Sputnik-1, but the result would be drastically different. Three seconds after the launch, the rocket began to lose its thrust, and after rising only a few feet up into the air, the rocket literally fell down and exploded, destroying the rocket and much of the launch pad. In the press, the mission was mockingly derided as "Stayputnik."

"Stayputnik"

The world was understandably impressed by the Soviets' successful Sputnik-1 and Sputnik-2 launches, including

American scientists. Americans opened the year 1958 hoping for a fresh start in the Space Race, but to get there, they first needed to reach the milestones set by the Soviet Union, much the same way the Soviet Union had to reach the milestones set by the Americans in the 1940s.

  On January 31, 1958, the United States proved that it, too, could launch a successful satellite into the Earth's orbit with the launch of the Explorer I satellite. While Explorer largely mimicked Sputnik's previous successes, it did make other contributions to space science. Explorer discovered the radiation belts that circle around the Earth's atmosphere, whereas Sputnik had only revealed information about the upper layers of the Earth's atmosphere.

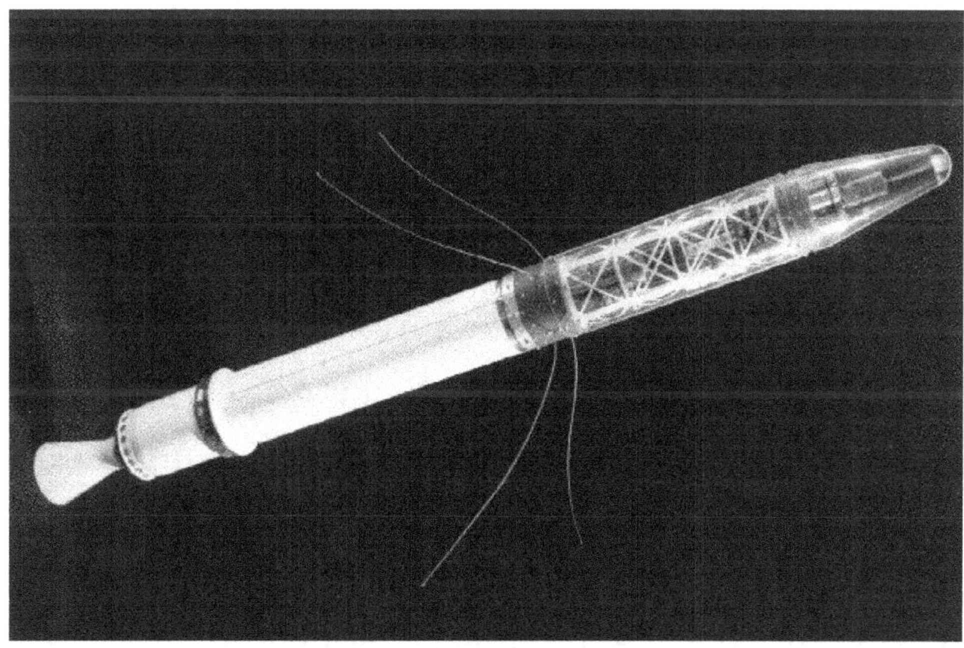

Explorer I satellite

In response to the success of Explorer I, the United States initiated the process of devoting greater national resources to space exploration. Up until 1958, all government space science was under the control of National Advisory Committee on Aeronautics (NACA). NACA, however, dated to 1915, and its original purpose focused on the realm of flight, not space. The department assumed space research after World War II, but it did so while also focusing on advancing flight. Its aims were expressly weapons-based. Put simply, NACA was to create weapons using the science of space and flight.

Although Project Vanguard was a failure, a "Redstone" rocket designed by von Braun had carried the first American satellite into orbit in early 1958, and later that year, Eisenhower formed the National Aeronautics and Space Administration (NASA). NASA's creation brought the disparate parts of the country's infant space program under one umbrella, one that clearly signaled that the United States' space program would be civilian, not military. However, due to the previous work done by the Army, Navy, and Air Force on rocketry, satellites, and the potential for manned space flight, the space program would continue to have a strong military component, because the rockets NASA could use to launch anything into orbit had their beginnings as ballistic missiles meant to carry nuclear weapons.

At the same time, after the launch that put Laika in space, the next natural milestone for both sides was to put a human into orbit. To date, the two sides had only put small objects into space, and in the case of Laika, aboard a small compartment with no intention of successfully landing. Launching a man into space and getting him back safely required significantly more technological advances.

The additional steps started with the Soviet launch of the Luna missions, which did not intend to launch a person or satellite into space. Instead, the Luna missions intended to explore the Earth's satellite, becoming the first spacecrafts to be launched toward the Moon. Naturally, launching an object into space at about 18,000 miles per hour and getting it to properly travel several days to the Moon was anything but easy. The first Luna was launched on January 2, 1959, but it missed its target by over 3,000 miles, thus flying right past the Moon instead of falling into its orbit as intended.

In September 1959, the Soviet Union launched the second Luna Mission, which culminated with Luna 2's landing on the moon, the first ever man-made object to touch the surface of the moon. Later in 1959, yet another Luna – Luna 3 – was launched, and with cameras onboard, the Soviets were able to take the world's first photographs of the far side of the Moon.

Luna 3

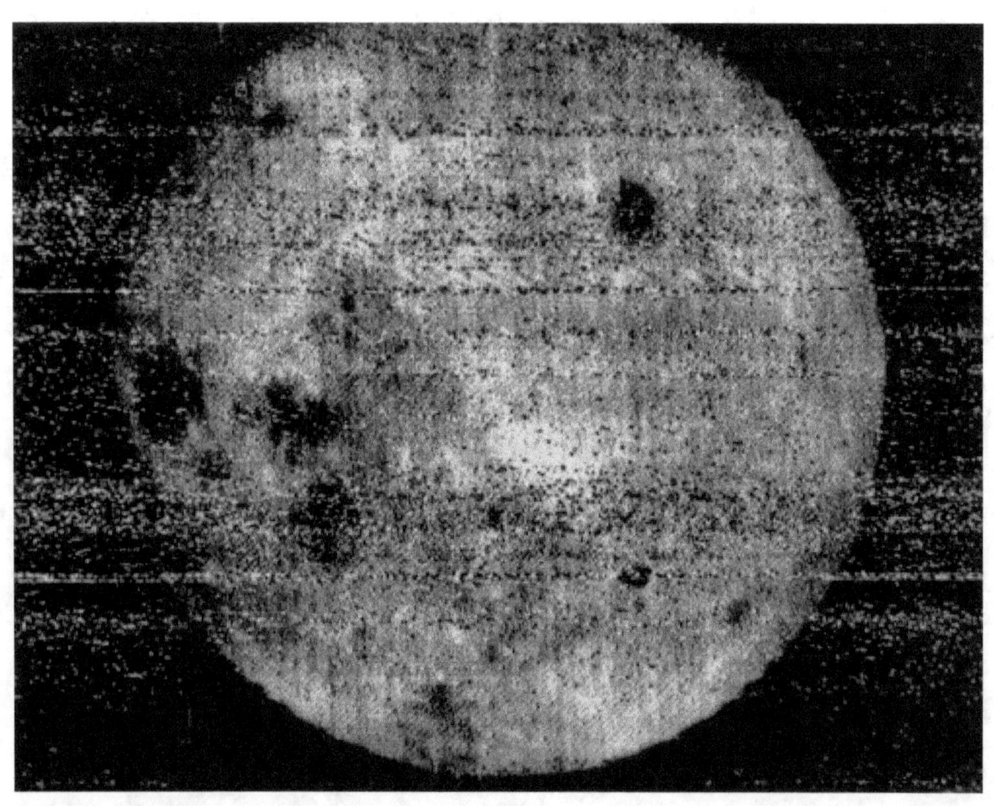

Luna 3's picture of the far side of the Moon

The Origins of Project Mercury

During World War II, Germany had taken the lead in the development of rocketry with weapons such as the *Vergeltungswaffe* 2 (V2 – Retribution Weapon 2), the very first long-range ballistic missile. No other country had similar technology, and as the war drew to a close, the Soviets and the Western Allies began a scramble to find and recruit scientists who had worked on the German rocket program. By that time, it had become apparent that rocketry would be a very important technology in the period after the war, and whoever was able to access Nazi technology would be able to kickstart their own rocket program.

The United States created the American Joint Intelligence Objectives Agency (JIOA) and gave it the dual objectives of identifying German scientists who might be persuaded to work for the United States while simultaneously ensuring that others did not fall into Russian hands. The American team working on this project were given a massive boost when a list of German scientists working for the Nazis, the Osenberg List, was found in a toilet in Bonn University. This allowed the Americans to identify potential targets, but for the Western Allies, the recruitment of Nazi scientists presented moral and ethical issues. President Harry S. Truman had specifically forbidden the recruitment of members of the Nazi Party, active Nazi supporters, or members of proscribed Nazi organizations, but given that membership of the Nazi party had reached almost 10 million by the end of the war and was practically a prerequisite for those who occupied senior positions, virtually all the Nazi rocket scientists were members of the party, which technically meant that none could be recruited to join an American rocket program. The agents of the JIOA found themselves in a very difficult position. They recognized that the early development of rocketry was essential to America's national interest, but the president's prohibition meant that they could not recruit the majority of German scientists because most had been members of the Nazi Party. The Soviets had no such qualms and were willing to recruit any scientist regardless of previous Nazi affiliations. Many people were concerned that this might give Russia a significant advantage in rocketry development.

To circumvent the president's prohibition, and without his explicit knowledge or permission, a secret decision was taken to whitewash the history of any rocket scientist willing to work for the US to remove any mention of Nazi Party membership or involvement in activities that might have led to imprisonment. This led to the wide-scale recruitment of German scientists regardless of their backgrounds, even though this meant concealing the truth from the American public. This program, which became known as Operation Paperclip, brought large numbers of German scientists to America immediately after the end of the war. These scientists became an important factor in the beginning of the American space program, and between March 1946 and September 1952, more than 60 captured German V2 rockets were launched from the White Sands Missile Range in a desolate area of sand dunes in southern New Mexico by the Upper Atmosphere Research Panel, the first official body established in America to work directly on rocketry. In 1948 and 1949, several of these launches included monkeys placed in the payload compartments of the rockets. None of the unfortunate animals survived the return to Earth, but the experiments seemed to prove that a large mammal would at least be able to survive the forces involved in the launch of a rocket.

None of these early launches represented true space flight, given that they were unable to reach sufficient height or speed to attain orbit. However, by the early 1950s, the US Army Ballistic Missile Agency (ABMA) began to look at whether the ballistic missiles it had developed as weapons could also be used for actual space flight. The ABMA, under the direction of von Braun, was given the task of developing the technology for this next step.

Even before the creation of NASA, work had already started on the biomedical research necessary before people could be sent into space. Around that time, the Working Group on Human Factors and Training was formed under the chairmanship of Dr. H. Guyford Stever from the Massachusetts Institute of Technology. This committee produced a report in October 1958 which became the basis for the NASA life sciences program, which was given the daunting task of looking at the biomedical, training, and selection procedures that would be required to ensure astronauts could survive and function efficiently in space. The Space Race is primarily remembered now for the advances it made in technology, but its biomedical aspects were just as significant and just as challenging.

Fortunately, the NASA life sciences program would not be starting with nothing, because by the time that this group was starting to look at the biomedical aspects of manned space flight, the US Army Air Force (which became the independent US Air Force in 1947) had already started research on the effects of high speed, high altitude flight on the human body. In October 1947 test pilot Captain Charles E. "Chuck" Yeager piloted the rocket-powered USAF-NACA X-1 to become the first person to officially fly faster than sound. In 1954, Lt. Col. John P. Stapp achieved a speed of over 600 miles per hour on a rocket-propelled sled as part of a USAF program to examine the effects of extreme acceleration and deceleration on the human body. In 1957, Maj. David G. Simons, a USAF flight surgeon, spent over thirty hours at an altitude of over 100,000 feet in the Manhigh II balloon.

Yeager

In July 1957, the USAF hosted a two-day conference which looked at the achievements of the US Air Force Scientific Advisory Committee in terms of possible space flight. The conclusion of the life sciences part of the conference was a belief that once a suitable launch vehicle and passenger capsule were developed, no further research into life sciences would be required for manned orbital flight. This was a bold assertion given that the USAF had included a number of animals in their missile launches, including mice and a South American squirrel monkey named "Old Reliable." At the time of the conference in 1957, none of these unfortunate creatures survived the flights (the USAF noted that Old Reliable survived the launch and flight without problems, but was killed following a "mishap" during reentry), so it was clear that a great deal of work was needed before a manned launch could be safely undertaken. With the creation of NASA, the USAF stopped research on manned space flight, but the information it had derived to that time was passed to the new agency.

Two members of the USAF who had been involved in biomedical research, Lt. Col. Stanley White and Captain William Augerson, were joined by a member of the US Navy space research program, Capt. Ashton Graybiel, a cardiologist and the Director of Medical Research, to form the aeromedical team of the newly created NASA Space Task Group. This group was given the task of examining the physiological effects of space flight and looking at the effects of zero-G, multiple-G, exposure to space radiation and potential exposure to matter from space on humans. Through this research, the team was expected to help plan a selection and training program for the first American astronauts.

By the late autumn of 1958, this project assumed an even higher priority when the Administrator of NASA said in relation to the first US manned space flight, "All right. Let's get on with it!" In September of that year, NASA and ARPA formed the Joint Manned Satellite Panel and before the end of the year this group had produced a report entitled "Objectives and Basic Plan for the Manned Satellite Project." This set out the overarching objectives for the US space program, with the most significant being the following: "To achieve at the earliest practicable date orbital flight and successful recovery of a manned satellite, and to investigate the capabilities of man in this environment."

This document went on to specify the basic requirements for life support, recovery, and emergency systems, as well as guidance systems, tracking capability, and ground support requirements. Although it was less than three pages long, this initial report was remarkably similar to what became the Mercury launch vehicle and capsule (even though the project as yet had no name), a remarkable achievement so early in the project and something that made subsequent development progress rapidly and without major changes to the basic specifications.

The document also set out three stages of testing that the program must work through. All the individual components of the spacecraft were to be tested separately as far as practicable, and then some form of testing of the completed vehicle would be carried out. Separately, pilot selection, evaluation and testing would determine the biomedical aspects of the planned flight.

The only rocket capable of launching the spacecraft was the Redstone, a rocket designed as an ICBM for the US Air Force by von Braun and his team and a direct descendant of the wartime German V2. However, it was clear that this rocket just didn't have the power required to launch a spacecraft into orbit, so it was accepted that early testing would involve sub-orbital flights and only later would a more powerful version of the Redstone, the Atlas, be available. Even then, the parameters chosen for the first manned orbit were very modest. The edge of the Earth's atmosphere lies around 2,000 miles above the planet surface, but there was simply no way that the technology of the late 1950s could be used to propel a manned capsule to that height. The Van Allen belt started at only four hundred miles from the surface, but even that was beyond the capacity of US rocket technology. Finally, it was agreed that the one-ton spacecraft would be launched to a maximum average altitude of just 100 miles above the Earth, the minimum required for a full 24-hour orbital trajectory. This also exceeded the fairly arbitrary Kármán line, the formal line that divided Earth and space, which was set at 62 miles above the surface of the planet. The main purpose of this line was to establish a border for Earth regulations and laws, but by exceeding it, these flights could at least be claimed to have met the legal definition of entering space.

The next issue facing NASA was what to call the new project. The earliest documents from NASA referred to the manned satellite program as "Project Astronaut," but there was a feeling that this name might focus too much attention on the human occupant of the craft rather than the technological progress being made as a whole. After a great deal of deliberation, a name was chosen that was rich in allegory and mythos: Project Mercury. Mercury, the son of Zeus and the grandson of Atlas, was chosen because it was felt that this god was well-known to the public and because the name had no military overtones.

Having chosen the name, the team began the design of the craft itself. The booster that would launch the vehicle into space would be derived from the new Atlas ICBM, though that was still undergoing flight-testing and would not be available for early test launches. The choice of Redstone for the early tests was also driven by cost considerations – NASA estimated that each Redstone launch would cost around $1 million, while an Atlas launch would cost more than twice as much. The development of Redstone-based craft for testing was given the title "Little Joe," while work on the final Atlas-powered manned vehicle was named "Big Joe." During 1959, design and development work on both craft accelerated.

As design work on the development of the technology progressed, the search for potential astronauts was still in its early stages. Some members of the team felt that the human inside the capsule was largely irrelevant, as most systems could be fully automated so that the astronaut would have relatively little to do. This group began to refer to the astronaut rather contemptuously as "spam in a can." However, the wider team recognized that the principle of manned space flight was important to establish. After all, while the Mercury orbital hops were relatively simple, later flights were already being considered that would be much more complex and would require the presence of several occupants in the craft.

Unmanned Launches

By August 1959, Project Mercury was ready for the first Little Joe launch. The contract for building the Little Joe rockets had been awarded to North American Aviation in

Los Angeles in January of the same year, and they worked as quickly as possible to meet NASA's demanding requirements for a series of test flights. Little Joe 1 (LJ-1) comprised a Redstone booster with a dummy Mercury capsule mounted on top. The purpose of this first launch was to test the Launch Escape System for the rocket – in the event of an aborted launch, a small rocket on top of the capsule would fire, hopefully taking the capsule and its occupant to safety. The launch was planned for August 21 at the Wallops Flight Facility on Wallops Island in Virginia.

A picture of the Wallops Island test facility

This first attempted Mercury launch was a complete failure. As the countdown was proceeding and the launch area was being cleared, there was an explosion on the craft. Later, it was determined that the Launch Escape System had triggered prematurely due to an electrical problem. Fortunately, no one was injured, but this was not the start that NASA wanted.

In October 1959, a second launch was attempted to test the escape system, and this went as planned. The following month Little Joe 1A was launched to test the escape system in high aerodynamic load condition, but this failed because the rocket motor for the escape system took too long to develop enough power to separate the capsule.

In December, the first launch of the spacecraft with a living occupant was tested, but this wasn't an astronaut. Sam was a rhesus monkey from the School of Aviation Medicine in San Antonio in Texas (his name was an acronym of the facility's title). Thankfully for Sam, the launch of Little Joe 2 went well and he and the capsule were safely recovered from the Atlantic Ocean. This was a very important milestone for the Mercury Program – they had proved that it was possible for a small mammal to survive the forces involved in a rocket launch and recovery. However, this was far from a true space flight – the maximum altitude achieved on this flight was around 55 miles above the Earth, well short of the altitude required to achieve orbit.

In January 1960, another rhesus monkey, Miss Sam, took part in the launch of Little Joe 1B, another test of the escape system. This too was a success and Miss Sam was safely recovered and returned to Wallops Island within forty-five minutes of the launch. All the Little Joe flights to this point had used dummy capsules, but the next, Little Joe 5, would be the first to test launch a real Mercury capsule.

This was another very important milestone for NASA, but before that flight, there was a test launch of the new and more powerful Mercury-Atlas combination. Launch MA-1 left the launch pad at Cape Canaveral on July 29, 1960, and the flight went as planned until 58 seconds after liftoff, when the Atlas rocket suffered a major structural failure and the craft crashed into the Atlantic and was destroyed less than three minutes later. This setback meant that LJ-5 would become the next attempt to achieve liftoff with a real Mercury capsule attached to the launch vehicle.

In January 1959 the McDonnell Aircraft Corporation had been chosen out of 12 bidders to build the Mercury spacecraft. The cone-shaped capsule had just one hundred cubic feet of pressurized habitable space inside, enough for only a single occupant. Although the capsule had a plethora of electrical systems, it did not have any on-board computers, which were still so large and bulky that it was not possible to fit them inside the small capsule. Instead, computers on the ground would carry out all the required computations and their results would be communicated to the astronaut in-flight by radio.

A picture of the production room at the McDonnell Aircraft Station

Capsule number 3 from the McDonnel production line was shipped to Wallops Island and testing and attachment to the Redstone booster progressed towards the original launch date in October. However, various problems and delays led to this being rescheduled for November 8, 1960, which happened to be Election Day that year. As incumbent Vice President Richard Nixon faced Senator John F. Kennedy, LJ-5 became the first flight in which a production capsule was tested in abort conditions at maximum dynamic pressure. Planning and preparation had taken almost an entire year, but while the flight left the launch pad on schedule, the joy lasted for all of 16 seconds. At that point, the escape rocket and the tower jettison rocket both ignited prematurely, while the Redstone booster was still producing full thrust. The capsule failed to separate and the booster and capsule were completely destroyed when they smashed into the Atlantic Ocean 13 miles from the launch pad.

This was a major blow to the program. Of the six Little Joe launches up to this point, only three were entirely successful, and worse was to follow. In tandem with the Little Joe test launches, another series of test flights for the Mercury-Redstone launch vehicle were planned to launch from the Cape Canaveral Air Force Station's Launch Complex 5. The first such mission, MR-1, had been scheduled for November 7 but was delayed due to technical problems. It was rescheduled for November 21 and, after the failure of LJ-5, NASA badly needed a success story. What it got was another public relations debacle.

The main engine of MR-1 ignited precisely on-schedule at 09:00 EST, but the rocket rose to a height of just four inches before the engine cut and the craft settled back gently on the launch pad. A few seconds later, for no apparent reason, the escape rocket fired and lifted itself to an altitude of 4,000 feet before crashing back to Earth. The capsule then deployed its drogue, main and reserve parachutes. Although neither the booster nor the capsule were seriously damaged in this accident, it did leave NASA with a potentially very serious situation – a fully fueled rocket was left sitting unsupported on the launch pad, and no one was quite certain what was going to happen. It was left in-situ until the following morning, by which time the on-board batteries were flat and it was safe to begin to dismantle it. What became known as the "four-inch flight" provided ammunition for those who were beginning to question the costs associated with space flight and asking whether NASA really had the expertise to achieve such ambitious objectives.

A picture of the failed launch

The answer came less than one month later with the launch of MR-1A, another Mercury-Atlas rocket carrying a real capsule on December 19, 1960. This time, the launch was a complete success. The spacecraft tested its instrumentation as well as guidance and retrorockets and safely splashed down in the Atlantic a little over 15 minutes after liftoff. Finally, it seemed that Project Mercury was making progress.

The Mercury Seven

As early as December 1958, NASA had drafted a civil-service job description for people who wished to apply for the position of "Research Astronaut-Candidate," and after meetings with industry and the armed services, it was agreed that an initial pool of 150 men would be selected. These would then be whittled down to a shortlist of 36 who would undergo tough physical and psychological testing before a final group of 12 would be put through a nine-month training and evaluation program. From these, just six would be chosen as the pool of astronauts for Project Mercury.

The requirements for reaching the first group of 150 were very stringent. Only men aged from 25-40 and less than 5'11 tall who had attained at least bachelor's degrees would be considered. In addition, successful applicants had to demonstrate one of five possible career/study backgrounds:

> At least three years of operational service in aircraft, balloons or submarines, as commander, pilot, navigator, communications officer or engineer, or,

> Completion of all requirements for a Ph.D. degree in any appropriate field of science or engineering plus at least six months of professional work, or,

At least three years of work in any of the physical, mathematical, biological, or psychological sciences, or,

At least three years of technical or engineering work in a research and development program or organization, or,

A medical degree with evidence of at least six months of clinical or research work beyond the license and internship or residency.

In addition, all candidates were required to prove that they had recently demonstrated:

"(a) willingness to accept hazards comparable to those encountered in modern research airplane flight;

(b) capacity to tolerate rigorous and severe environmental conditions; and

(c) ability to react adequately under conditions of stress or emergency."

The document went on to explain, "These three characteristics may have been demonstrated in connection with certain professional occupations such as test pilot, crew member of experimental submarine or arctic or antarctic explorer. Or they may have been demonstrated during wartime combat or military training. Parachute jumping or mountain climbing or deep sea diving (including SCUBA) whether as occupation or sport, may have provided opportunities for demonstrating these characteristics, depending upon heights or depths obtained, frequency and duration, temperature and other environment conditions, and emergency episodes encountered."

If these weren't enough to deter all but the most determined applicants, each person was also required to provide endorsement of their application by a "responsible organization."

As it turned out, NASA's complex planning for astronaut selection was undermined before it even began, because during Christmas 1958, President Eisenhower intervened personally. He pointed out that the US Air Force, the US Navy and the Marine Corps already had a large pool of experienced and qualified test pilots, so he questioned why the astronauts for Project Mercury could not be selected from amongst these men. Although many people in NASA were concerned and dismayed at the notion that future astronauts could only be taken from the military, they were forced to concede that this would greatly simplify the selection process. Thus, a meeting at NASA in early January 1959 agreed that Air Force, Navy and Marine test pilots were a good potential source of astronauts, and a new, simplified, eight-point selection list was drawn up. Suitable candidates had to meet the following criteria:

1. Aged less than 40.

2. Less than 5 feet, 11 inches tall.

3. In excellent physical condition.

4. Holding a bachelor's degree or equivalent.

5. A graduate of test pilot school.

6. Having 1,500 hours total flying time.

7. Qualified jet pilots.

The specification no longer noted that applicants had to be male, but this was simply because all the current test pilots were men. The idea that an astronaut could be female was not something that seems to have occurred to NASA or any of the other bodies involved. A review of Air Force and Navy personnel records revealed at least 100 men fit the new criteria, and it was agreed that the initial group of potential astronauts who would be subject to training and evaluation would be drawn from this group.

In the wake of announcing Project Mercury in December 1958 with the explicit mission of launching a man into orbit and return him safely to Earth, NASA asked the

Bureau of Aeronautics to send a test pilot to their Langley Research Center in Hampton, Virginia, then the location of the Space Task Group, to make runs on a spaceflight simulator. The same pilot would go to the Naval Air Development Center in Pennsylvania for runs in a centrifuge, which would be used for comparison with the simulator data. John Glenn requested the position, and permission was granted for him to participate. He spent several days at Langley and at the centrifuge, and according to a 2007 article in the Smithsonian Institution's *Air and Space Magazine*, "John Glenn called it a 'dreaded' and 'sadistic' part of astronaut training...The centrifuge's flight simulation capabilities made it possible to reproduce all the ways various spaceflight scenarios could affect astronaut performance. 'We did the early Mercury training of John Glenn and [Wally] Schirra and all the rest of those guys just to learn what happens if we go up to these sorts of accelerations in these different vectors,' Shender says. 'We were talking about reentry and during takeoff, long-term exposures. So if we're going to develop these ballistic profiles, how much can people take? It was a great unknown.' For the Mercury, Gemini, and Apollo astronauts, the 'wheel' was both a rite of passage and an invaluable training tool. 'Whirling around at the end of that long arm, I was acting as a guinea pig for what a human being might encounter being launched into space or reentering the atmosphere,' Glenn recalled…'You were straining every muscle of your body to the maximum…if you even thought of easing up, your vision would narrow like a set of blinders and you'd start to black out.'"

Glenn

Schirra

69 men were summoned to the Pentagon in February 1959 for further evaluation and a briefing on Project Mercury from NASA. After culling the pool down some more, the agency subjected the 32 candidates who remained to a series of grueling physical and psychological tests at the Lovelace Clinic in Albuquerque

and the Wright Aerospace Medical Laboratory in Ohio.
From the 18 candidates who remained after this round of
testing, Robert R. Gilruth, head of NASA's Space Task
Group, selected seven men as the first American
astronauts.

Gilruth

John Glenn, Scott Carpenter, Gordon Cooper, Gus
Grissom, Wally Schirra, Alan Shepard, and Deke Slayton
were introduced to the world in a press conference in
Washington, D.C. on April 9, 1959. The *Associated Press*,
following NASA's lead, hastened to shape the reputation

of America's new heroes, writing on April 10, "Seven jet pilots in their 30s--family men all—faced a challenging future today as newly assigned Mercury astronauts. Their mission: to ride satellites in orbits around the earth at altitudes of 100 to 150 miles and speeds of 18,000 miles an hour— and to bring themselves safely home again…At a National Aeronautics and Space Administration news conference Thursday the astronauts analyzed their' assignments with cool detachment. The work would be difficult, they said, but not too dangerous. Were they worried? Hardly. Did their families approve? Heartily. Were they happy about it? Delighted to get on the team. From the relative obscurity of military jet flying, the seven were catapulted into the status of public figures."

The article also pointed out that the "oldest" of the astronauts was "its lone Marine, Lt. Col. John Herschel Glenn Jr., 37, New Concord, Ohio," reminding the public about Glenn's "first supersonic-all-the-way transcontinental flight." It then described the team: "Each of the astronauts has two children except for Carpenter, with four, and Slayton, with one. As they strode onto the stage of the NASA auditorium in their first public appearance, they were an impressive group. All are slender, well-groomed, neatly dressed in conservative suits, white shirts and dark ties. Their heights range from 5 feet 10 to 5 feet 11, except for Cooper, 5 feet 9'/2 and

Grissom, 5 feet 7. Their weights range from 150 pounds for Cooper to 185 for Schirra. All seven are white and Protestants. All emphasized their wives endorsed the new careers, and that those of their children old enough to understand were enthusiastic about it...As for the reaction of the wives Glenn said he could not have entered the program "if I didn't have good backing at home—my wife's attitude is the same as it has been through all my flying that what I want is all right."

  Dr. Randolph Lovelace, who headed the selection team, reported that "the volunteers went through the most rigorous selection program ever devised. The test simulated conditions of heat, cold, noise, stress, acceleration and deceleration that might be encountered in real space flight. They were conducted largely at the Lovelace clinic and at the Aeromedical Laboratory at Wright-Patterson Air Force Base, Ohio."

Grissom, Shepard, Carpenter, Schirra, Slayton, Glenn and Cooper in 1962

It quickly became clear to everyone that Glenn was the star of the group. As Tom Wolfe later wrote, Glenn "came out of [the press conference] as tops among seven very fair-haired boys. He had the hottest record as a pilot, he was the most quotable, the most photogenic, and the lone Marine." The truth of the matter was that Glenn had plenty of help from NASA, which shaped the image of the astronauts as all-American Cold Warriors. The Mercury Seven were all carrying the hopes of country's manned space program on their shoulders, and the magnitude of the task before them was made starkly clear when, a few weeks later, they were at Cape Canaveral to watch their first rocket launch. The rocket, an Atlas very similar to one that would carry the astronauts into orbit, exploded a few minutes after takeoff. Watching the spectacle in stunned silence, Alan Shephard turned to Glenn and said, "Well, I'm glad they got that one out of the way."

Shepard in his Freedom 7 space suit

During the second half of 1959, all the astronauts went through punishing training at several centers across the country. Part of the issue was that no one was entirely sure what physical and psychological issues astronauts would have to deal with. This was compounded by a lack of suitable training equipment. Each man had to learn to use and operate in the bulky pressure suits being developed at the Goodrich plant in Akron, Ohio while being subjected to intense sessions in a massive centrifuge at Johnsville in California and undergoing heat stress training and exposure to high levels of carbon dioxide. In addition, each astronaut was expected each week to complete at least three hours of flying, four hours of athletics, and six hours of study in their specialist areas. As if all that wasn't enough, all the astronauts were also given survival training in case the capsule descended into a remote area, including learning to survive in a desert or jungle.

The astronauts also became involved in the design and development of the spacecraft. For example, in May 1959, all seven were brought to the McDonnell Aircraft Corporation laboratories and factory and allowed to inspect the mockup capsule. All expressed concerns about the poor visibility from two small portholes and the difficulty of climbing into and out of the capsule through a small opening in the top. As a direct result, the capsule was redesigned to provide better visibility and access through a new and larger hatch.

Meanwhile, national interest in the astronauts was so high that, with the encouragement of NASA (which also had a statutory duty to provide educational material), the seven sold the rights to their stories to Time Life, Inc. for $500,000 (worth around $4.5 million today). Some people were horrified at this agreement to pay active-duty military officers for their stories, but the feeling in NASA was that this money would provide for the families of the astronauts if something terrible happened to them. It was agreed that this payment would be equally divided amongst the seven, regardless of who was the first in space, because that was something that still had not been decided. Clearly, there was going to be a great deal of kudos for the first American in space and members of the team confidently assumed that this person would also be the first man in space, something that would go down in history as a giant step for all of mankind.

Plans for the first manned Mercury sub-orbital flight progressed during 1960 and the first such launch was scheduled for November. However, delays in the completion of Mercury capsule 7 by McDonnel meant that this was revised to mid-January 1961, and the failure of the MR-1 launch in November 1960 caused further delays while systems were checked and rechecked. The public and many newspapers began to express concern at delays in the program and to ask whether NASA really had the expertise required. One headline article in a well-regarded weekly defense industry trade journal, *Missiles and Rockets*, was titled, "Is Mercury Program Headed for Disaster?" By the end of the year, *Time* was complaining about the "lead-footed" Mercury program and noted of the failed MR-1 launch, "Project Mercury's latest failure, third in a row, just about evaporated the last faint wisp of hope that the U.S. might put a man into space before Russia does." Ominously, G. Pokrovsky, a member of the Soviet Academy of Science, claimed around that time, "We are on the threshold of manned space flight, and the first man to be in space will undoubtedly be a Soviet citizen."

  Progress was finally made on the last day of January 1961 when another Mercury-Redstone launch, MR-2, was made with a living occupant in a real capsule: a chimpanzee named Ham. Despite problems and technical hitches, the launch went well and Ham was safely recovered, and if a chimpanzee could survive a sub-orbital flight, it seemed certain that a human could too. This success was reinforced on February 21 with the successful unmanned launch of another Mercury-Atlas craft, MA-2. At the beginning of April 1961, work began on the erection of the spacecraft for what was planned to be the first manned flight: MR-3.

Project Mercury seemed to be making good progress towards that goal when the United States received another shock on April 12, 1961, the day the Soviets launched Yuri Gagaran into space for a flight that took the Russian slightly more than once around the Earth. Much the same way the Soviets had beaten the United States into space with Sputnik, they had beaten them again. No one was surprised when the *Associated Press* reported that "to America's three would-be astronauts the news brought disappointment. Each of the American trainees had hoped to be the world's first man to soar into outer space. Most vocal of the three was Lt. Col. John Glenn." The article went on to quote Glenn as saying, "The Russian accomplishment was a great one. It was apparently very successful, and I am looking forward to seeing more detailed information. I am naturally disappointed that we did not make the first flight to open this new era. The important goals of Project Mercury, however, remain the same. Ours is peaceful exploration of space."

Gagarin's mission into space was part of the Soviet Vostok program, which had been preceded by several more Sputnik missions meant to test the feasibility of human space travel. Sputniks 4 and 5 were particularly helpful. Both sent a human-sized mannequin into space, along with various other mammals – first a guinea pig, then a dog – to test the possibility of sustaining life in space. The last mission successfully launched and de-orbited the animals successfully, although one of the dogs suffered a seizure on the fourth orbit of the Earth, leading the Russians to determine that a human should only orbit three times. With that, the groundwork was paved for the Vostok 1 mission to send a living human being into space and back.

The Vostok Module

The Sub-Orbital Manned Flights

Another Mercury launch took place on April 25, 1961, but instead of carrying a human passenger, the spacecraft contained a crew simulator, an electronic mannequin that could "inhale" and "exhale" while being monitored for temperature and other parameters. Although the team at NASA were very keen to catch up in the space race, it was not felt that testing was sufficiently complete to safely include an astronaut on this flight. Ultimately, that proved a wise decision, because 40 seconds after liftoff, the automatic control systems on the Mercury-Atlas craft malfunctioned and the booster was deliberately destroyed by the ground controller. However, the capsule escape system worked as planned and the capsule was safely recovered with the crew mannequin intact.

By this time, three astronauts among the Mercury Seven had been selected for the first manned flights: John Glenn, Gus Grissom, and Alan Shepard. Even before Gagarin's historic flight, Shepard had been selected as the first to take part in a manned Mercury launch, MR-3, and for this flight a tradition was established that would be followed for the rest of the Mercury Program – the selected astronaut was allowed to name the spacecraft. This craft used Mercury capsule number seven, and Shepard chose the name "Freedom 7" for the craft.

The flight was scheduled for Tuesday, May 2, but bad weather caused a last-minute cancellation and the flight was delayed for 48 hours. Then, the weather forecast on that day meant the flight was rescheduled for Friday, May 5. Public interest in the flight was huge and only increased when the name of the astronaut taking part was released on May 2. Some people were so concerned at the possibility that the flight might fail that it was suggested the launch be conducted in secret and the public informed only if and when it was successfully accomplished. It was decided that this was not appropriate and that American taxpayers had the right to see what their money was being spent on.

  By the time of the launch, more than 350 foreign and domestic news representatives had registered with NASA to cover the event. The countdown began at 8:30 p.m. on May 4 and everything went without a hitch. On the morning of May 5, 1961, an estimated 45 million Americans tuned in to watch a live television broadcast from Cape Canaveral where Freedom 7 sat on top of a black-and-white Redstone booster. At 9:34 a.m. local time, the countdown finally ended and the rocket lifted smoothly from the launch pad. Millions watching on television heard Shepard as he made radio calls to the flight control center: "Ahh, Roger; lift-off and the clock is started . . . Yes, sir, reading you loud and clear. This is Freedom 7. The fuel is go; 1.2 g; cabin at 14 psi; oxygen is go . . . Freedom 7 is still go!"

  The media and the American public celebrated as America had finally placed a man in space, but objectively this did not begin to measure up to the technical achievement of Gagarin's flight. While the Russian spacecraft had achieved orbit, the first manned Mercury flight was a simpler sub-orbital hop, straight up and straight back down again. The entire flight lasted just 15 minutes and Shepard was standing on the deck of the aircraft carrier USS *Lake Champlain* less than 30 minutes after liftoff. The flight was entirely successful and achieved its main aim of confirming that the Mercury craft was capable of taking a man safely into space and recovering him afterwards.

Perhaps more importantly, Alan Shepard had also performed as planned. He had been weightless for around one-third of the total flight time and medical examinations on board the Lake Champlain seemed to show that he had suffered no ill effects from this or from the acceleration or vibration of the launch and flight.

Less than 3 weeks later, on May 25, 1961, President Kennedy addressed Congress to discuss the importance of the Space Race within the context of the Cold War. The speech remains famous because he spelled out his vision of landing a man on the Moon before the decade was over:

> "First, I believe that this nation should commit
> itself to achieving the goal, before this decade is
> out, of landing a man on the Moon and returning

him safely to the earth. No single space project in this period will be more impressive to mankind, or more important for the long-range exploration of space; and none will be so difficult or expensive to accomplish. We propose to accelerate the development of the appropriate lunar space craft. We propose to develop alternate liquid and solid fuel boosters, much larger than any now being developed, until certain which is superior. We propose additional funds for other engine development and for unmanned explorations--explorations which are particularly important for one purpose which this nation will never overlook: the survival of the man who first makes this daring flight. But in a very real sense, it will not be one man going to the Moon--if we make this judgment affirmatively, it will be an entire nation. For all of us must work to put him there…

   "Let it be clear--and this is a judgment which the Members of the Congress must finally make--let it be clear that I am asking the Congress and the country to accept a firm commitment to a new course of action, a course which will last for many years and carry very heavy costs: 531 million dollars in fiscal '62--an estimated seven to nine billion dollars additional over the next five years. If we are to go only half way, or reduce our sights in the face of difficulty, in my judgment it would be better not to go at all.

"Now this is a choice which this country must make, and I am confident that under the leadership of the Space Committees of the Congress, and the Appropriating Committees, that you will consider the matter carefully.

"It is a most important decision that we make as a nation. But all of you have lived through the last four years and have seen the significance of space and the adventures in space, and no one can predict with certainty what the ultimate meaning will be of mastery of space.

"I believe we should go to the Moon. But I think every citizen of this country as well as the Members of the Congress should consider the matter carefully in making their judgment, to which we have given attention over many weeks and months, because it is a heavy burden, and there is no sense in agreeing or desiring that the United States take an affirmative position in outer space, unless we are prepared to do the work and bear the burdens to make it successful. If we are not, we should decide today and this year. "

A picture of Kennedy giving the speech

While that would change the trajectory of Project Apollo, which was still in early planning, it was still essential that Project Mercury achieve its aims in order to accrue the data needed for the much more complex and challenging Apollo missions. Moreover, planning for the next sub-orbital Mercury mission assumed a new significance.

On July 15, 1961, it was announced that Gus Grissom would be the astronaut for the next Mercury-Redstone flight, MR-4. Grissom took the name Liberty Bell 7 for the craft, and modifications were made both to the capsule and the space suit Grissom would wear following lessons learned from Shepard's flight. The mission was planned for launch on July 18, but, just as with MR-3, weather problems caused delays. The flight was rescheduled to the 19th and then again to the 21st. Finally, at 7:20 a.m. on Friday, July 21, Liberty Bell 7 left the launch pad at Cape Canaveral.

The short flight went perfectly up to the point where helicopters from the aircraft carrier USS *Randolph* arrived to collect both Grissom and Liberty Bell 7 from the ocean. The capsule's escape hatch was explosively ejected before the helicopter was able to winch it higher in the water (Grissom was certain that he hadn't touched the jettison lever and believed that the hatch had malfunctioned). Water immediately began flowing into the capsule. Grissom was able to scramble out into the water, but, almost at the same moment, the rescue helicopter hovering overhead developed engine trouble and had to return to the carrier, leaving the second helicopter to take over. Within moments, the Mercury capsule sank in almost 3,000 fathoms of water, and for a short time it looked as though Grissom might follow it. While the space suit was designed to stay afloat, but it was losing air fast and Grissom was having a great deal of trouble keeping his head above water. Fortunately, the helicopter was able to lower a personnel hoist and Grissom was winched aboard, but it had been a close call and the precious capsule was lost in the deep water.

Despite a major investigation, the cause of the premature hatch jettison was never solved. Some people in NASA believed that Grissom had inadvertently hit the release lever, but he remained adamant that he had not. On top of that concern, additional pressure was applied to NASA when news arrived that Russia had successfully completed a second manned mission when cosmonaut Gherman S. Titov stayed in space for more than one day and achieved more than 17 complete orbits. This made the sub-orbital hops of the Mercury-Redstone flights look meager by comparison, and it was clear that NASA must soon place an American astronaut in orbit if it was to retain its credibility.

Friendship 7

The flight of the Vostok spacecraft carrying Titov caused particular concern in America because three of the flight's 17 orbits had taken it directly over the United States, and the notion that a Russian Air Force officer could fly over the country led to a great deal of discussions. One of the obvious conclusions was the perception of "space-lag," the belief that America was falling behind in the race with the USSR. Several additional Mercury-Redstone missions had originally been planned, but the low power of the booster meant that these could never be anything but more sub-orbital hops. It was believed that NASA needed to accelerate its program, and on August 18, 1961, it released an announcement that the Mercury-Redstone project had successfully achieved all its objectives and was therefore terminated. All future Mercury missions would involve the more powerful and complex Mercury-Atlas rocket, but unbeknownst to most, that rocket was proving difficult to refine.

Even as NASA was announcing the end of Mercury-Redstone, a Mercury-Atlas rocket was on the launch pad at Cape Canaveral. MR-4 was planned as an unmanned orbital mission carrying a "crew simulator" electronic mannequin. This would be the fifth Mercury-Atlas launch, and there was no avoiding the fact that three of the previous launches had been partly or completely unsuccessful. The purpose of MR-4 was to prove that the Mercury-Atlas rocket could place a man in orbit and recover him safely, and there were plenty who still doubted that NASA had the ability to achieve that objective.

The launch of MR-4 was originally planned for August 21, but the discovery of technical problems during pre-launch testing meant that the spacecraft had to be removed from the launch gantry and returned to the hangar for refurbishment. Bad weather (including the arrival of two hurricanes) caused further delays, so it wasn't until September 13 that MR-4 was finally ready to go. At 9:04 a.m. it left the launch pad on its single-orbit mission. There were some issues, but it successfully completed the planned orbit and a little less than one and a half hours after liftoff, the spacecraft fired its retrorockets and began the reentry procedure. A short time later it splashed down in the Atlantic east of Bermuda and was recovered by the destroyer USS *Decatur*.

Examination of the capsule at NASA revealed some minor problems with the oxygen system and with faults caused by vibration, but otherwise the craft had performed as expected. At a press conference, NASA officials explained that this had been the most complex and challenging American space flight to date and that its success was a very positive development. Reporters eagerly asked whether the next Mercury-Atlas flight would be a manned mission, but it was explained that more test flights were required first.

The unmanned Mercury-Scout mission was planned to launch on October 31, primarily as a means of testing and refining the Mercury tracking system. The countdown proceeded smoothly, but when it reached zero, nothing happened. The electrical circuits controlling the ignition system had failed, so they were repaired and the countdown was resumed the following day. This time, the craft lifted off the launch pad but, just 28 seconds into the mission, the booster began to behave erratically and tore itself apart.

The next launch, MA-5, was scheduled for November, and precisely what the craft would contain was up in the air until nearly the very end. The original plan had been to send up a chimpanzee on a multi-orbit mission that would replicate the planned first manned orbital mission, but some within NASA felt that this was overly cautious and that the American people needed to see an astronaut in orbit before the end of 1961. The debate was settled when the failure of Mercury-Scout confirmed that further testing was needed.

The sole occupant of MA-5 was a chimpanzee named Enos, and to the enormous relief of everyone involved, the mission was nearly flawless. MA-5 completed a single orbit of Earth before the capsule descended into the Atlantic and was recovered by the destroyer USS *Stormes*. The capsule and Enos were carefully examined and both were pronounced to have fared well. There now seemed to be no reason to delay the first manned orbital flight.

Although it was never formally acknowledged, it does seem that NASA tried to rush the launch of MA-6 to ensure it took place before the end of 1961, but it quickly became apparent that technical problems meant that this was impossible. On December 7 (the anniversary of the Japanese attack on Pearl Harbor), it was announced that MA-6 would launch in early 1962, and in early January 1962, NASA announced a planned launch date of January 23. The agency confirmed that John Glenn would be the astronaut involved.

Glenn served as the backup pilot for the Shepard and Grissom flights, but he had been selected as the top choice for Mercury-Atlas 6, America's first manned orbital flight. Glenn named his Mercury capsule Friendship 7, and along with his backup pilot, Scott Carpenter, Glenn undertook hours of training in static and simulator tests, flying 70 simulated missions and responding to 189 simulated failures.

Delays bedeviled Glenn's attempt to become the first American to orbit the Earth, but Friendship 7 finally lifted off on February 7, 1962 after 11 delays due to equipment malfunctions and weather issues. The flight was not uneventful - after the first orbit, during a 30 minute test to see if Glenn could fly the spacecraft manually, the automatic control system failed. Glenn recalled, "I went to manual control and continued in that mode during the second and third orbits, and during re-entry. The malfunction just forced me to prove very rapidly what had been planned over a longer period of time."

Pictures of Glenn entering the spacecraft before the launch

The launch

More concerning to ground controllers was a telemetry reading that indicated that the head shield had loosened. If this reading was accurate, Glenn and his spacecraft would inevitably burn up on reentry. Ground control told Glenn not to jettison the retrorocket pack before reentry, as they believed the pack would keep the heat shield in place, but they did not tell Glenn about the heat shield readings since nothing could be done about it at that point anyway.

The pack broke up on reentry, and Glenn observed the flaming chunks of debris flying past the window during reentry. A 2012 article on Space.com quoted Glenn as saying "there were flaming chunks of the retro-pack burning off and coming back by the window. I didn't know for sure whether it was the retro-pack or the heat shield, but there wasn't anything I could do about it either way, except just keep trying to work and keep the spacecraft on its actual best attitude coming back in." Glenn later remarked to an interviewer that "fortunately it was the rocket pack—or I wouldn't be answering these questions."

After the flight, NASA engineers determined that the reading had been caused by a faulty sensor and not a loose heat shield. Steve Lindsey later admitted, "His odds of not surviving this was about one in six. So it was an extremely high-risk, unknown effort that they were going into, having never done it before."

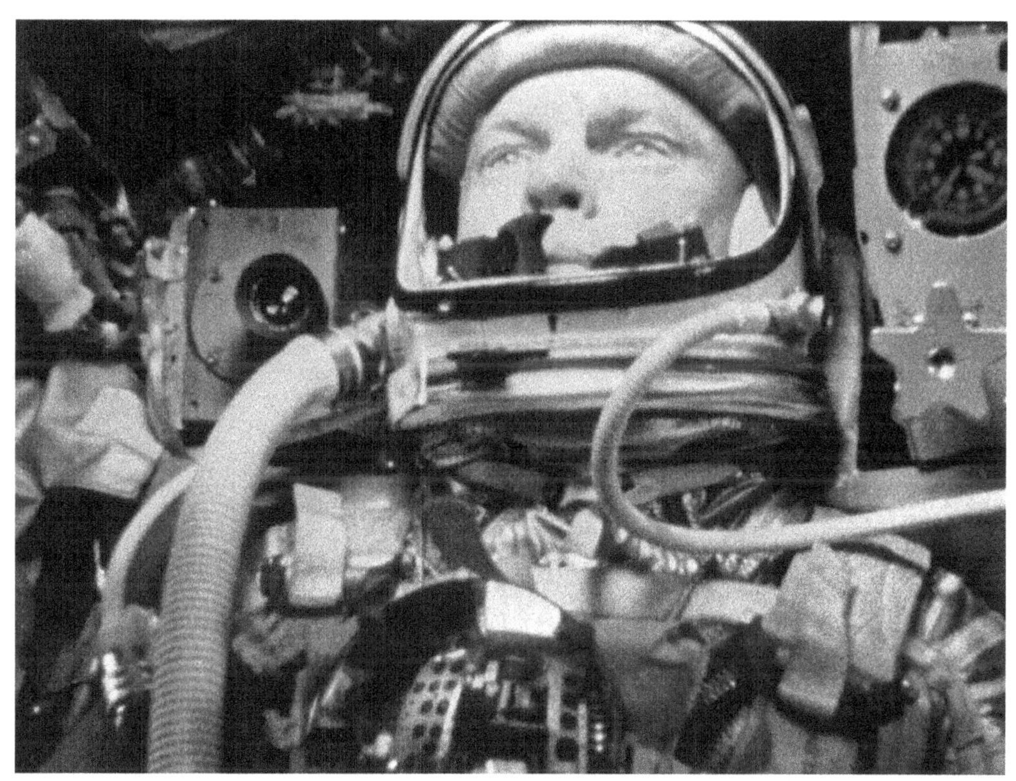

A picture of Glenn in orbit

A photo taken by Glenn during the mission

After a three-orbit flight which took 4 hours and 55 minutes, Friendship 7 safely splashed down 800 miles southeast of Cape Canaveral. In the event that he landed thousands of miles off course in the South Pacific, he carried a note in several island languages that read, "I am a stranger. I come in peace. Take me to your leader and there will be a massive reward for you in eternity." Fortunately, the note was not necessary, and Glenn, having traveled 75,679 miles at 17,500 miles per hour in a flight that took him to a maximum altitude of 162 miles, landed well within his target zone. Glenn was plucked from the Atlantic by the recovery ships and taken back to the mainland.

By the time he was back, he was no longer merely an astronaut or Marine Corps aviator. As the first American to orbit Earth, the third American in space, and the fifth human in space, Glenn was a certified hero, and he called the mission the "best day of his life." In addition to being a personal triumph; it renewed American confidence and put the world on notice that the United States was in space to stay.

**The Friendship 7 capsule now on display at the
National Air and Space Museum in Washington**

The flight also united the nation in a way that few non-war related events ever could. The *Associated Press* reported, "Americans of every political shade and social scale were united today in cheering a single man who had carried their hopes to the stars and had written another chapter in the human adventure. The man was LI. Col. John H. Glenn Jr.—an individual of a nation of individuals. He was in his space capsule all alone, but 180

million hearts beat with his, and Americans throughout
the land had joined in a single prayer: 'Please, God, let
him make it.' During the flight business workers,
government officials and just plain people dropped
everything to follow the proceedings. Stores emptied.
Kitchens were deserted. Telephone conversations were cut
down markedly, schoolchildren were given their current
events lesson via television and radio. In Reno, Nev.
gamblers quit the gaming tables. President Kennedy arose
to watch the preparations on a TV set, then phoned Cape
Canaveral to make a personal check on the situation.
Congress all but halted its deliberations as legislators
watched a portable TV sot to see the progress of
America's first representative to outer space. In New York
City, 5,000 commuters stood In Grand Central Terminal
to watch the rocket firing on a huge, television screen.
There wore shouts of 'Thank God' and 'He made It' when
word was received that Glenn had been picked up."

  Glenn naturally received a hero's welcome. Shortly after
the mission, in a ceremony at the Manned Spaceflight
Center in Houston, President Kennedy awarded Glenn the
NASA Distinguished Service Medal. Upon receiving the
medal, Glenn told those present, "I can't express my
appreciation adequately to be here accepting this when I
know how many thousands of people all over the country
were Involved in helping accomplish when we did last

Tuesday and knowing how particularly this group at the Cape and many of the group here on the platform and our own group of astronauts who were scattered all around the world and who performed their functions at the Cape also. We all acted literally and figuratively as a team and it was a real team effort all the way. We have stressed the team effort in Project Mercury. It goes across the board, I think—sort of a crosscut of Americans, of industry and military and civil service, government work, contractors…I would like to consider that I was sort of the figurehead for this whole big tremendous effort and I'm very proud of this medal I have on my lapel here for all of us—you included—because I think it represents all of our efforts—not just mine." Glenn also received a ticker-tape parade in New York City, joining the ranks of another aviation pioneer, Charles Lindbergh. In addition, the Marine Corps awarded him his sixth Distinguished Flying Cross for his flight.

A picture of Glenn being honored by Kennedy

Glenn's fame was not without its downside. Kennedy took a personal liking to Glenn, seeing in the astronaut great symbolic and political value, both of which he desperately needed in the wake of the Bay of Pigs fiasco. Kennedy skillfully wrapped himself in Glenn's fame, saying, "In the last 24 hours we have seen facilities now being created for the greatest and most complex exploration in man's history. We have felt the ground shake and the air shattered by the testing of a Saturn C-1 booster rocket, many times as powerful as the Atlas which launched John Glenn, generating power equivalent to

10,000 automobiles with their accelerators on the floor."

According to NASA administrator Charles Bolden, since Glenn was now a celebrity, Kennedy would not "risk putting him back in space again." At 42, he was the oldest member of the astronaut corps, and he would be 50 by the time of the Apollo flights. Even had he not been the first American to orbit the Earth, it was always likely that the lone mission in Project Mercury would be the only one of his career, and as it turned out, the groundbreaking orbital flight would be Glenn's last trip into space for over 30 years.

The End of Project Mercury

With the success of mission MA-6, Project Mercury had fulfilled its primary purpose to develop the technology and systems required to send a man into orbit and recover him safely, but the project itself still had more to achieve. Though Glenn's flight had been successful, certain technical issues seemed to suggest that more pilot control over the spacecraft was a good idea. When astronaut John Carpenter lifted off on mission MA-7 on May 24, 1962, he was in a redesigned and reworked capsule named Aurora 7. He was able to perform a number of new experiments, including using the additional control systems, but when he splashed down, errors in retro-rocket firing meant that he was some distance from the planned splashdown area.

Carpenter spent almost three hours floating in a life raft before he was rescued by a helicopter from the aircraft carrier USS *Intrepid*. Fortunately, he was just fine and the capsule was also recovered without difficulty.

Walter Schirra was selected as the astronaut for the next Mercury mission, MA-8, a longer six-orbit flight that would reach a higher altitude than either Glenn or Carpenter. After some delays, MA-8 launched on October 3, 1962, and once again, millions of Americans settled down in front of their televisions to watch live coverage of the flight. They were able to listen in as Schirra spoke to mission control and joked about being able to see both the United States below him and the Moon in the distance at the same time. The mission was a complete success and the capsule, Sigma 7, splashed down precisely where planned, in full view of the waiting ship's crews and ecstatic news cameramen. Nearly 10 hours after liftoff, Schirra and the capsule were winched aboard the carrier USS *Kearsarge*.

In May 1962, NASA launched the most ambitious mission yet, an extended flight of at least 18 orbits, which required a major redesign of many components of the tiny craft. On the morning of May 15, MA-9 lifted off carrying astronaut Gordon Cooper in capsule Faith 7. 34 hours and 20 minutes later, the spacecraft splashed down precisely as planned after completing 22 orbits. Both the craft and the astronaut were recovered safely by the *Kearsarge.*

Though no one at NASA knew at the time, MA-9 would be the last Mercury mission. There were plans for at least one more mission, MA-10, but rising costs and a feeling that Project Mercury had achieved all it could do meant that the mission never took place, and in June 1963, NASA formally announced that there would be no more Mercury missions.

By then, Project Gemini (originally named Mercury II) was well in hand, and these missions would work on launching a much larger, two-man spacecraft on the even more powerful Titan II rocket. Even though Project Gemini was almost two years away from its first launch, it made sense to focus all NASA's funds and energy on those missions and the Apollo plans rather than to continue with Project Mercury.

The week after Project Mercury was officially terminated, the Soviet Union launched Vostok V, and cosmonaut Valery F. Bykovsky achieved 81 orbits. Just two days later, Valentina V. Tereshkova became the first "cosmonette" in Vostok VI, which achieved 48 orbits. Project Mercury had allowed America to regain lost ground in the Space Race, but it was clear that the country was still well behind the Soviets' space program.

The Mercury Seven went on to follow varied careers. John Glenn retired from NASA in 1964 and from the USMC in 1965. He went on to pursue a career in politics, becoming the U.S. Senator for Ohio. However, his career in space didn't end with the Mercury flight, because in 1998 he flew in the Space Shuttle on mission STS-95 as a civilian payload specialist. At the age of 77, he remains the oldest person to have been in space.

In 1963, Alan Shepard was diagnosed with Ménière's disease, which temporarily ended his career as an astronaut. He remained with the space program as Chief of the Astronaut's Office, and after corrective surgery, he was able to resume operations and went on to become the commander of Apollo 14. He was the fifth and oldest man to walk on the Moon.

Gus Grissom went on to command a Gemini mission and was appointed the commander of Apollo 1 before he was killed in a fire in the Apollo 1 capsule during a launch rehearsal.

Malcolm Scott Carpenter never flew in space again after his participation in the MA-7 flight. He was injured in a motorcycle accident and left NASA in 1967. He retired from the US Navy in 1969 with the rank of Commander.

Gordon Cooper flew in space as part of one of the Gemini missions in 1965. He retired from both NASA and the US Air Force in 1970 with the rank of Colonel.

Schirra. went on to fly missions for Gemini and Apollo, becoming the only astronaut to take part in all three of the main NASA programs. He retired from both NASA and the US Navy in 1969 with the rank of Captain and joined CBS News, where he became one of the presenters covering the Apollo Moon landings.

Donald Slayton was the only one of the Mercury Seven not to undertake a flight during the project. During training, it was discovered that he suffered from a minor heart condition, so he was grounded as a result. He retired from the US Air Force in 1963 with the rank of Major but remained with NASA and eventually became Director of Flight Crew Operations. He was returned to flight status in 1970, and in 1975 he took part in the last flight of an Apollo spacecraft as part of the Apollo-Soyuz Test Project. He retired from NASA in 1982.

The Future

After the last Mercury flight, it wasn't until March 1965 that the first manned Gemini flight left the launch pad at Cape Canaveral with Gus Grissom as pilot in command, joined by a new astronaut, Ed White. Gemini would consist of 10 manned launches in a little over 18 months.

New developments included the first Extra-Vehicular Activities (generally known as "spacewalks") and, in December 1965, the first in-space rendezvous between spacecraft when Gemini 6 and 7 were able to adjust their orbits to float in space less than one foot apart.

All the while, as the Gemini missions were making headlines and producing some truly astonishing images, the focus of NASA was already switching to what had become its main target: placing a man on the Moon. Project Apollo suffered a major setback in January 1967 when a catastrophic fire inside the Command Module tragically killed astronauts Gus Grissom, Ed White, and Roger Chaffee during a launch rehearsal. After that disaster, no manned space flights were undertaken until the first manned Apollo mission in October 1968.

Apollo had been given added impetus after President Kennedy was assassinated in November 1963. Kennedy had committed the US to placing a man on the Moon "before this decade is out," and fulfilling that vision would require all kinds of work before culminating in the historic Apollo 11 mission in July 1969. Between that time and the last Apollo Moon mission in December 1972, six successful missions placed 12 astronauts on the Moon and brought them all safely back to Earth, and with that, America had effectively won the Space Race. Though NASA had plans for bases on the Moon and manned missions to Mars, public interest in space flight was declining and many people criticized the vast amounts of money needed to support these programs. The space program was drastically cut back and, after the last Apollo flight in 1975, the only major program to receive funding was what became known as the Space Shuttle project for a reusable spacecraft. From 1981-2011, Space Shuttles designed and developed by NASA flew more than 130 missions.

   With the end of the Space Shuttle program on 2011, America temporarily abandoned manned space flight. American astronauts are still launched into space to spend time in the International Space Station (ISS) but, ironically, they are launched into space on Russian Soyuz rockets. The only manned space flight programs currently ongoing in the US are those being pursued by private corporations. Virgin Galactic has developed SpaceShip2 (SS2), a re-useable craft intended to promote commercial space tourism.

   Despite the hiatus, NASA may soon be back in the business of manned spaceflight. In 2017, President Donald Trump signed Space Policy Directive 1, authorizing funding for a new NASA program named Artemis. This program has the goal of placing "the first woman and the next man" on the Moon before the end of 2024. The first (unmanned) launch of the new Orion spacecraft is scheduled for November 2021, and it has even been suggested that the Orion spacecraft may be used for manned Mars missions, perhaps in the 2030s. With these developments, it seems that the manned space flights that began with such optimism during Project Mercury may soon resume.

Conclusion

The challenges faced by NASA and the Mercury Seven were huge. Before the project, there was no certainty that a person could withstand the rigors of spaceflight and no knowledge of whether the technology available in the 1950s and 1960s would enable it safely. The project was made even more demanding because it was carried out in the glare of public interest and scrutiny, and during heightened competition with the Soviet Union. Mercury answered questions in the most emphatic way and led directly to the following Gemini and Apollo missions. The Gemini and Apollo craft were more advanced and much more complex than the Mercury spacecraft, but their development used lessons learned from Mercury. Mercury did not win the Space Race for America, but it made eventual victory possible and helped to restore confidence in US science and technology.

While Mercury was eventually a success story, the project came at an enormous cost. Most estimates suggest Mercury cost up to $400 million. In addition to NASA personnel, the project involved 12 main contractors, 75 secondary contractors, and more than 7,000 subcontractors, as well as Defense Department personnel involved in supporting individual missions. It is estimated that at its peak, more than two million people were working directly on or for Mercury. Given these numbers, the costs are unsurprising.

  NASA learned some important lessons thanks to the missions, most significantly the importance of having astronauts with all kinds of capabilities for dealing with contingencies. Before the Mercury flights, some people took the view that the human passenger in a spacecraft was little more than an observer with little to do in a largely automated craft, but Mercury made clear that astronauts would play an important role in actually flying the craft, something that was incorporated into the design of the later Gemini and Apollo spacecrafts. Mercury also accomplished more than its technical achievements suggest, because the project helped America and the Western world look to space for the first time as a location for exploration. In 1965, Hugh Dryden, NASA Deputy Administrator, succinctly summed up the impact of Project Mercury: "The events of the last seven years have had profound impact on all human affairs throughout the world. Repercussions have been felt in science, industry, education, government, law, ethics, and religion. No area of human activity or thought has escaped. The toys of our children, the ambitions of our young men and women, the fortunes of industrialists, the daily tasks of diplomats, the careers of military officers, the pronouncements of high church officials - all have reflected the all-pervading influence of the beginning steps in space exploration."

There is no doubt that Project Mercury brought about a philosophical change that pervaded society in America and beyond, but there is a small commonplace postscript to the story that can be found on the shelves of virtually every hardware store in America and around the world. The Atlas rocket that was used to launch Mercury capsules had fundamental problems - it was too large to be stored inside most hangars and its thin metal skin was prone to corrosion when it was exposed to water. A small research company in California, the Rocket Chemical Company, set out to create a chemical compound that would both disperse water and protect the rocket from corrosion. After 39 unsuccessful attempts, they finally created something that worked: Water Dispersant (WD) Formula 40. This was used to treat the Atlas rockets of Project Mercury, and in 1959, the company began selling an aerosol version of this compound commercially as Rocket WD-40. By 1993, it was estimated that four out of every five households in America had at least one can of WD-40, and it remains the most popular water dispersant and anti-corrosion treatment in the world. Those distinctive yellow and blue cans continue to provide modern societies with a direct link to the pioneering technology of Project Mercury.

Online Resources

Other books about space by Charles River Editors

Other books about Project Mercury on Amazon

Further Reading

Alexander, C. C.; Grimwood, J. M.; Swenson, L. S. (1966). This New Ocean: a History of Project Mercury (PDF). US: NASA. ISBN 1934941875.

Cassutt, Michael; Slayton, Donald K. "Deke" (1994). Deke! U.S. Manned Space: From Mercury to the Shuttle (1st ed.). New York, US: Forge (St. Martin's Press). ISBN 0-312-85503-6.

Catchpole, John (2001). Project Mercury - NASA's First Manned Space Programme. Chichester, UK: Springer Praxis. ISBN 1-85233-406-1.

Gatland, Kenneth (1976). Manned Spacecraft (Second ed.). New York: Macmillan. p. 304.

Giblin, Kelly A. (Spring 1998). "Fire in the Cockpit!". American Heritage of Invention & Technology. American Heritage Publishing. 13 (4). Archived from the original on November 20, 2008. Retrieved March 23, 2011.

Grimwood, James M. (1963). Project Mercury. A Chronology – NASA SP-4001. Washington DC, US: NASA. Retrieved November 8, 2015.

Hansen, James R. (2005). First Man: The Life of Neil A. Armstrong. Simon & Schuster. ISBN 0-7432-5631-X.

Kranz, Gene (2000). Failure is not an option. New York, US: Berkley Books. ISBN 0-425-17987-7.

Nelson, Craig (2009). Rocket Men: The Epic Story of the First Men on the Moon. New York, New York: Viking Penguin. ISBN 978-0-670-02103-1.

Siddiqi, Asif A. (2000). Challenge To Apollo: The Soviet Union and the Space Race, 1945-1974 (PDF). US: NASA. ISBN 1780393016. Archived from the original (PDF) on September 16, 2008.

Unknown (1961). Results of the first U.S. manned sub-orbital space flight (PDF). US: NASA.

Unknown (1961a). Results of the second U.S. manned sub-orbital space flight (PDF). US: NASA.

Unknown (1962). Results of the first United States manned orbital space flight, 20 February 1962 (PDF). US: NASA.

Wilford, John Noble (July 1969). We Reach the Moon. New York, US: Bantam Books.

NASA. "Computers in Spaceflight: The NASA Experience - Chapter One: The Gemini Digital Computer: First Machine in Orbit". NASA History. NASA. Retrieved September 15, 2016.

Rutter, Daniel (October 28, 2004). "Computers in space". Dan's Data. Retrieved September 15, 2016.

"Space flight chronology". IBM Archives. IBM. Retrieved September 15, 2016.

"IBM 701 – A notable first: The IBM 701". IBM Archives. IBM.

Free Books by Charles River Editors

We have brand new titles available for free most days of the week. To see which of our titles are currently free, click on this link.

Discounted Books by Charles River Editors

We have titles at a discount price of just 99 cents everyday. To see which of our titles are currently 99 cents, click on this link.